OUR LIFE IS PREDETERMINED

CHENBAGAM PILLAI

INDIA • SINGAPORE • MALAYSIA

ISBN 979-8-89066-777-9

CONTENTS

DESCRIPTION

These days subjects like Kundalini Awakening, The Wisdom or the Truth, Third Eye, and various Breathing Techniques which are mainly related to Yoga are often written about by many people with different opinions.

The main cause for the difference of opinion is that there are no particular references, like books and verses to quote from, to confirm their writings.

One and only source for the above subjects is ancient manuscripts like the Scriptures and Arts irrespective of religion and region.

Truth is one and there will not be more than one Truth whether in the East or West. Language and culture cannot bar the Truth.

The main obstacle to understanding the manuscripts is that they are full of proverbs, parables, similes, etc. Sometimes, it is called a Mystic Work which cannot be understood by ordinary people.

Mystic words are called 'Pari Pasha or Substitute.' Nowadays, most people do not know that the book 'Pari Pasha' is also available as a dictionary for understanding the meaning of the words. In the same period when the manuscripts were written, the book of Pari Pasha was also written by scholars.

Ancient Tamil scholar Thirumular said that every one of the scriptures has two meanings — 'common and special.' Ordinary people do not know and will not accept this, but the scholars will accept it.

> "வேதம் ஆகமங்கள் இறை நூலாம் வேதம் ஓதும் போது பொது
> மற்றும் சிறப்பு பொருள் உண்டு
> வேதம் ஓதும் போது இரண்டு அர்த்தம் பேதமே என்பர் சிறியோர்
> பெரியோர்க்கு அபேதமே"
>
> – *Thirumular – Thirumanthiram.*
>
> *"Veda and Agamas are about the Gods. There were two meanings for the verses – special and common. Ordinary people will not accept it but the scholars will."*

Fortunately, the author had both ancient manuscripts and the book of Pari Pasha. So in this book, each and everything has been explained with the original verses, art etc. Explaining the world through symbols, statues, paintings etc., are very common in ancient manuscripts. In this book, mystic words have been demystified with the help of Pari Pasha.

Here, Tamil manuscripts have been mainly used to understand the real meaning of the scriptural words. Anyway, in the same way, anyone can understand the scriptures in their mother language.

"Truth is bitter". So, our ancestors didn't want to write everything for all. Innocent people may feel sad after reading the same. Because the illiterate are living a happy life by thinking of real as unreal and unreal as real It is the cause for them (scholars) to use the mystic words...

Anyhow, the people who are interested in knowing the Truth, can use the substitute words (Pari Pasha) to get the benefit of understanding the manuscripts which are available in their region and language.

"Art is worth more than a thousand words".

Lady Justice:

- Blindfold, dagger, double-edged sword, scale, etc.
- Blindfold: It represents impartiality and fair treatment for all.
- Dagger: It signifies the punishment for guilty without any leniency.
- "When justice is done, it brings joy to the righteous but terror to the wrongdoers." – Proverb.
- Scale: It is clear evidence of either balance or imbalance.
- Some other weapons are goad, trident, bow and arrow, lash etc.

Life imitates art far more than
art imitates Life.

When justice is done, it brings joy to the righteous but terror to the wrong doers" - proverb

Another important thing is "The Five."

Five elements – Earth, Fire, Water, Air and Sky

Five senses – Eye, Nose, Ear, Tongue and Skin

Five letters – Na Ma Si Va Ya

Five levels of Kundalini Raising.

Pancha Bootham
(Five Elements)
It is the real cause
of sound and
breathe.

Five Koshas

- Anna mayam (Digestive system)
- Prana mayam (Generation of vital energy from the lower part of the abdomen – that is the seat of Kundalini.)
- Vingana mayam (Changes in body chemistry)
- Mano mayam (Changes in mind)
- Ananda mayam (Attaining the blissful state)

There are many arts in the world such as sculptures, paintings etc., to explain the Truth.

Breathing pattern

- Left nostril, right nostril and both nostrils
- left nostril breath means the body is in cool condition -Parasympathetic Nervous System works more.
- Right nostril breath means the body is in hot condition – Sympathetic Nervous System, and when the breath goes through both nostrils, it means our body is in normal condition – Central Nervous System.

Our body is itself in the process of changing the breathing pattern depending upon our body's requirements.

The food we eat, Physical and Mental activities will frequently change the pattern.

As per the law of nature "Weekly Schedule" would happen without any outside interference. When it goes out of control, it will be dangerous for our general health.

Our ancient scholars have studied this wonderful natural mechanism within us well, and have written it in poetic form under the heading of "Vara Charam" – Weekly String.

After realizing the importance of the theory, they decided to record it permanently in all forms. Their main choices are in written form, sculptures, paintings etc. Temple was considered the right place for this.

Anyone can see these things wherever they look at the temple. Every nook and corner of the temple will expose these great truths.

Pillars, corridors, doors, and walls are some examples. Even the Temple Tower which is full of colourful sculptures is nothing but explaining the Truth.

There are many rules to doing this job. For that purpose, they have created the "Agamam" – the rules for building the temple. So, we can see the same thing without any modification of structures in almost all the temples.

For the same reason, almost all big temples have two important sites: one is "Maha Mandabam" – "The Great Hall" and the other is "Artha Mandabam" – "Meaningful Hall", which is full of sculptures.

The temple tower is also built in the same concept as the right and left hemispheres.

> "ஊனுடம்பே ஆலையம், உள்ளமே பெரும் கோவில்".
>
> *Meaning is that*

Our body is like a shrine and our mind is like a big temple.

The temple tower is full of sculptures which explain the same. They are not simple dolls.

Pancha Bootham
Response to
the
Balance

One can see that many sculptures are in nude form.

It is not what we call "Obscene".

Here, nude means what is within us (spirit or Soul), not the outward physical body which is a temporary subject.

Temples were built under the supervision of the king and religious leaders. Without their knowledge, no one could make such nude sculptures. It was allowed because there was a purpose in it.

Temples are full of sculptures some nude structures and others about God and goddess forms.

In the same way, in the western world, paintings were made. Ancient artists have made their work with an impression (formless) that everything in the world has no form – impermanent. The formless has been explained and showed as nudes.

"What spirit is so empty and blind, that it cannot recognize the fact that the foot is more noble than the shoe, and skin more beautiful than the garment with which it is clothed?" – Michaelangelo.

He who says God exists, for him it is existing. He who says there is no God, for him it is not.

According to Hermetic principles, we are just mind, which is no form but formless. The mind will go wherever it wants to go. It is like a flying object.

Clothes or attire is for outward showing. It is no use for life (inside). When life is not, what is the use of the clothe?

As the saying goes, *"God is in pillar and even in particles"*.

The verses, rhythmic poems, chanting mantra and Bajan like chorus singing are written for the same purpose – to recognize the meaning of the words.

" யான் பெற்ற இன்பம் பெறுக இவ்வையகம்" -

"Yan petra Inbam peruga Ivyagam..."

– Thirumular

Meaning is that each and everyone in this world should enjoy the happiness that I have enjoyed.

Also, the book has given many symbols, pictures, and words for the benefit of readers who are interested in gaining more knowledge about the same.

Some text, verses, and even pictures may be repeated at various places which is necessary for understanding.

Ancient manuscripts were passed to disciples from the Guru as oral, not in written form. So, these days no one can write any scriptures like the ancients.

The knowledge of Vedas helps us to see the changes within our body which cannot be seen by any other available tools.

Also, it would be helpful to face any crisis at any place and time.

All scriptures or ancient scholars insist that we see inside of us. Though it is very difficult, if one can see then he would be free from worldly sufferings.

"The intelligent person will go inward first. Before going anywhere else, you will go into your own being. That is the first thing, and it should have the first preference. Only when you have known yourself can you go anywhere else. Then wherever you go will carry a blissfulness around you, a peace, a silence, a celebration."

– Osho

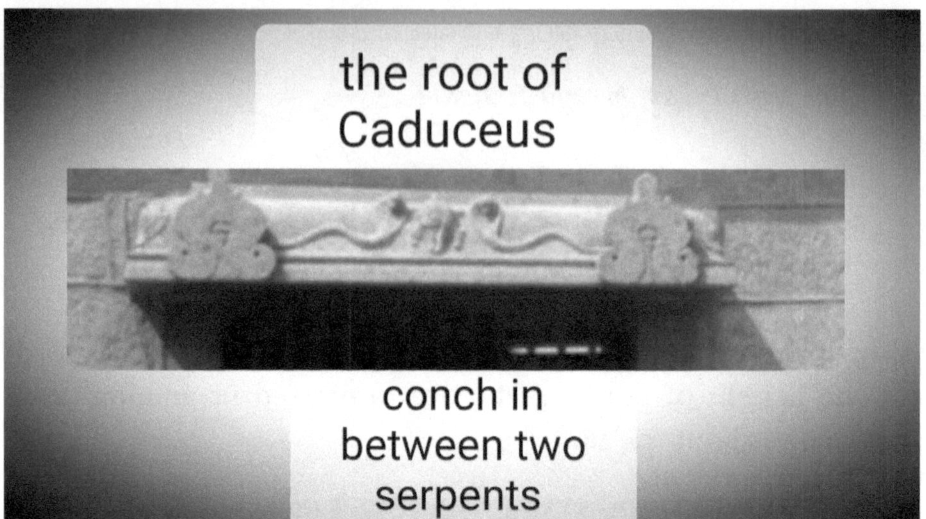
the root of
Caduceus
conch in
between two
serpents

1. THREE NATURAL LAWS AS

Circadian Clock

Seven Hermetic Principles,

Seven days law and He, She and It Principles

Three important principles were followed by ancient scholars to understand Nature and its relation to human beings.

Circadian Clock

The modern world has more ideas about this principle than what has been proved by modern science. Recently, the prestigious Nobel Award was given to scientists for their proof of this theory.

An important factor of this principle is that all living beings respond to this effect.

That is, our body recognises daytime and night with the changes of light and dark. It can be observed and followed by all living beings including animals and plants.

While all living bodies strictly and unknowingly follow the law, we as human beings do not follow and it is one of the causes for our health issues.

The 7 Hermetic Principles

1. **The principle of mentalism**
   All is mind; Universe is mental.

2. **The principle of correspondence**
   As is above, so below; as below, so above.

3. **The principle of vibration**
   Everything rests; everything moves; everything vibrates

4. **The principle of polarity**
   Everything is dark; everything has poles;
   everything has its pair of opposites

5. **The principle of Rhythm**
   The pendulum – "swing in manifest everything"
   the measure of the swing to the right is
   the measure of the swing
   to the left; Rhythm compensates.

The subjects like Circadian clock and Hermetic principles have already been written about by many authors.

So other subjects like "Seven Day Law" and "He, She and It" – will be explained here.

Seven Day Law

(Weekly Schedule of Breathing Nostrils)

– *Ancient Tamil manuscripts*

(Here, Thirumular's verses have been mentioned)

1. Seven days law

It starts from the

Sun

Earth

Day and night

Five elements

Earth, fire, water, air and sky.

A month

15 days from the waxing moon and 15 days from the waning moon

Fire + water = air (vapour or spirit)

The air or vapour which rises to the atmosphere, after condensation, comes down to earth as water.

This is happening continuously to maintain life on Earth.

The above process has been explained by science, we know. But here, it is gaining importance because, we are going to understand the subject with the help of ancient scholars.

–the same thing is happening within us.

As is above, so is below.

What is happening outside is also happening inside.

What is in an atom, that is in the universe.

> ***"Still God pours the rain from the sky and gives life to the dead earth. It is also the best proof of his presence."***
>
> ***– from an ancient manuscript.***

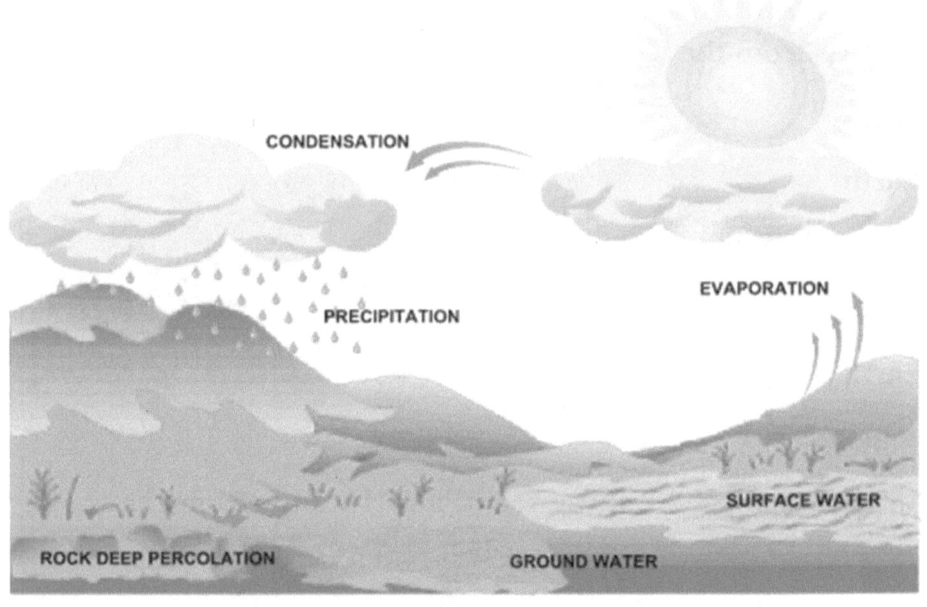

Breath Rhythm in Days of the Week

On different days of the Week, breath Rhythms differ between the left and right nostril.

> "வெள்ளி வெண் திங்கள் விளங்கும் புதனிடம்ஒள்ளிய மந்தன்
> இரவிசெவ்வாய் வலம வள்ளிய பொன்னே வளரும் பிறையிடந்
> தெள்ளிய தேய்பிறை தான் வலமாமே.
>
> *On Fridays, Mondays and Wednesdays,*
> *Prana dominates in the nadir or nostril that is to the left. On*
> *Saturdays, Sundays and Tuesdays*
> *It courses high in the right;*
> *On Thursdays*
> *Prana flows in the left*
> *In the waxing moon's fortnight;*
> *And in the right in the waning moon's fortnight.*

"வெள்ளிவெண் திங்கள் விளங்கும் புதன் மூன்றுந் தள்ளி
யிடத்தே தயங்குமே யாமாகில் ஒள்ளிய காயத்துக்கு
ஊனமில்லையென்று
வள்ளல் நமக்கு மகிழ்ந்துறைத் தானே."
"செவ்வாய் வியாழஞ்சனி ஞாயிறே என்னும்
இவ்வாறு அறிகின்ற யோகி இறைவனே
ஒவ்வாத வாயு வலத்துப் புரியவிட்டு
அவ்வாறு அறிவார்க்கு அவ்வானந்தமே
நடுவு நில்லாமல் இடம் வலம் ஓடி
அடுகின்ற வாயுவை அந்தணன் கூடி
இடுகின்ற வாறு சென்றின் பணி சேர
முடிகின்ற தீபத்தின் முன்னுண்டென்றானே.".

The prana runs helter and skelter
To Right and to Left;
If Yogi gathers it proper
And regulates to reach Kundalini,
He shall stand before the Infinite Light;
Thus, He said before the Infinite Light;
Thus, He said, Nandi Holy.

'பழமை எனப்படுவது யாதெனின் யாதும் கிழமையைக்
கீழ்ந்திடா நட்பு.'

– Thirukural

The Old Practice is nothing but following the rules of breath (Seven-Day Law) without fail, as mentioned in the Vedas.

'நாள் தோறும் நாடி முறைசெய்யா மன்னவன்
நாள் தோறும் நாடு கெடும்.'

– Thirukural

Meaning is that

He who does not follow the breathing rules as per day of the week will lose his health.

above sculpture represents that left side as female and right side as male.

2. "HE, SHE AND IT"

"அவன் அவள் அது என்னும் அவை மூவினையில் தோன்றிய திதியே ஒடுங்கி மலத்துளதாம் அந்தம் ஆதி என்மனார் புலவர்."

– Siva Ghana Botham

Meaning is that
The universe is made by He, She and It.....

– Siva Ghana Botham......
– Saint Meykanda Nayanar.

He – அவன் – ஆண் – நெருப்பு – Sun – +ve charge
She – அவள் – பெண் – நீர் – moon – -ve charge
அது – (product produced by the water and fire) – vapour, spirit, life force, body's vital energy.

Arthanarisvarar

(meaningful of
Male and
Female)

(Nari - female
Easwar - Male)

The Kundalani energy or Sakthi - female force is the real cause of all actions.

Figure 1: He She It

> “நாபியின் கீழே நல்லதோர் எழுத்துண்டு பாவிகாள் அதன் பயன் அறிவாரில்லை ஓவியராலாலும் அறிய வொண்ணாது தேவியும் தேவனும் திகழ்ந்திருந்தாரே”
>
> – *Thirumular – Thirumanthiram*

It (lower abdomen – Mulathara is a birthplace of all sounds or vibrations which generate the vital energy) helps in the act of breath retention and raising the energy from below the navel region. It is a rare art that helps the practitioner to advance on the Yoga path.

"கடைவாசலைக் கட்டிக் காலை எழுப்பி
இடை வாசல் நோக்கி இனிதுள் இருத்தி
மடைவாயிற் கொக்கு போல் வந்தித்திருப்பார்க்
உடையாமல் ஊழி இருக்கலாமே."

Bind the Moolathara
Raise the Prana breath upward
Through the Spinal canal, course it
And within in aptness retain,
And like a stork at stream ahead
Sit calm
In singleness of thought;

Well, may you live forever and ever.

Figure 1: Temple car with Sun and Moon wheels

He, She and It.
the temple tower

the temple car -
it's wheel
represents the
Sun and the
Moon.

3. THE WISDOM OR THE TRUTH

> *"Wisdom is not a product of schooling but of the lifelong attempt to acquire it."*
>
> *– Albert Einstein*

The same Wisdom was obtained by Swami Vivekananda from Sri Ramakrishna Paramahamsa.

King Arjuna got it from an experienced sage with the advice of Lord Krishna.

Buddha got the Truth from his own experience. Sri Ramana Maharishi got it from his own experience.

மெய்ஞ்ஞானம் – உண்மையான அறிவு

(The real knowledge about the physical body and subtle body)

"உடலால் அழியில் உயிரால் அழிவர்
திடம்பட மெய்ஞானம் சொன்னாலும் கேட்கவும் மாட்டார்
உடலை வளர்க்கும் உபாயம் அறிந்தே
உடல் வளர்த்தேன் உயிர்
வளர்த்தேனே"

– Thirumular – Thirumanthiram

Means that one who doesn't maintain a healthy body would lose his life. And even if it was told to them, they wouldn't listen to the truth about the body and its relation to life (life force). I have known the Truth and so I lived a long, healthy life.

"எப்பொருள் யார் யார் வாய் கேட்பினும் அப்பொருள் மெய்ப்பொருள் காண்பது அறிவு"

– Thiruvalluvar

Who said it is not important, but how one interprets and understands it's real meaning is.

"Believe nothing, no matter where you read it or who has said it, unless it agrees with your own reason and your own common sense."

– Buddha

"I am the Light, I am the Truth and I am the Way."

– from Scripture.

The word Truth has been mentioned in all popular scriptures.

The subject of The Truth has been discussed worldwide from time immemorial to the present day.

From Bhagavat Geetha,

Just before starting the war, King Arjuna hesitates to start the war. He said to the Lord Krishna, "Just because of getting the kingdom, I do not want to kill the people who are all my relatives and my own people. It is better to go as a beggar instead of killing these innocent people."

At that time, Lord Krishna said, "It is not a good practice for a king like you. It is your duty to save your innocent people from bad ruler.

Lord Krishna said to King Arjuna, I "If Arjuna, you should know the Truth or Wisdom. After getting the knowledge, then you need not want to know anything of this world and need not worry about anything which is happening in the world. The same knowledge (the highest knowledge) will relieve you from the present agony." Here, Lord Krishna did not say what is the knowledge but advised King Arjuna to go to an experienced sage to get the knowledge of Wisdom.

The Wisdom or the Truth is a highest knowledg in the world.

The knowledge will help us to come out from the illusionary world.

Buddha was a king. He ruled and lived a happy life in the palace with his wife and children.

But his mind was always wavering about three things – old age, disease and death.

He enquired about it from scholars from his country and even outside of his country. But he didn't get the right answers from all these sources.

He didn't have enough time to think over this because of his commitments as a ruler of the country and a head of his family. So he decided to go to the jungle just for the solitude. He spent a few years and suffered a lot.

But one day, when he was sitting under the peepal tree (one of the important subjects for gaining knowledge of Wisdom) and got the answer to his questions.

Then, he returned home and again lived a satisfied life.

But once, when his wife asked him about knowledge (Wisdom) if it is not possible to get Wisdom from here itself. He answered that it is possible, but I couldn't confirm it because his mind was engaged in different things.

When the mind is still and stable, breathing will be calm and the body becomes stable and healthy. The mind is the controller of all the senses. When all the senses are in control, one can feel the inner peace.

Illusion is a word used to refer to that one who appears to be unaware of what is happening. He perceives both the real and the unreal as being true, since his mind was programmed to think in this way since childhood.

So, if we desire to discover the Truth, we must set aside everything we have already learnt.

Many sages liked isolation and silence because they could assist them in achieving their goals.

How did Buddha get enlightened?

Buddha tried for six years, but he could not reach. Then he dropped the desire to become enlightened and the same night he got enlightened and his enlightenment came when he became desireless.

But if you look deep, he became obsessed with it and he dropped the very idea of getting enlightened. What we learn from here is – desireless.

When Buddha was asked about his experience after enlightenment,

he replied, 'Nothing'. However, Buddha said, let me tell you what I lost: Anger, Anxiety, Depression, Insecurity, Fear of old age and death.

Enlightenment is seeing the Brahman or Brahma who resides in you. That is also called as Nirvana. When you see him, there is nothing left to be seen. When you know him there is nothing left to be known. In Tamil language, Nirvana means nude.

Our life is considered a physical body and a subtle body Philosophically, nude or nirvana is a subtle body. It is called as soul, self, etc.

> "தன்னை அறிய தனக்கு ஒரு கேடில்லை
> தன்னை அறியாமல் தானே கெடுகின்றான்
> தன்னை அறியும் அறிவைதான் அறிந்தபின்
> தன்னையே அர்ச்சிக்கத் தானிருந்தேனே."

– *Thirumular*

He spoils himself without knowing himself
He did not try to know himself
I am after knowing myself
I worshipped me.

"If the disguise started in the body, when the body dies, then the disguise will also die.
He who does not realize the truth of life is like a log caught in the sea."

The principle that is Uniting the physical body and the subtle body is called Yoga. Without knowing this knowledge of yoga, there will be no use for doing yoga.

Anyhow, it is a knowledge.

Ancient scholars insisted that there is no knowledge above this in this world.

Here, are some parables which are used in the Scriptures to interpret and realise the Truth.

"இரவும் பகலும் மாறி மாறி வருவதை நீ பார்க்கவில்லையா? அறிவுள்ளவனுக்கு இதில் அத்தாட்சி இருக்கிறது"

– *Quran*

"Haven't you seen the day and night come successively. He who is intelligent can get the proof."

– *from Scripture.*

"இரவுக்கு 12 மணிநேரம், பகலுக்கு 12 மணிநேரம் என்பது உங்களுக்கு தெரியாததா?

– *from Scripture.*

"Don't you know that the night has 12 hours and the daytime has 12 hours a day?".
"He himself makes the Sun and the moon for the sake of you."
– from Scripture

வேதம் ஓதினும் வேதம் விளங்கிடா
வேதம் ஓதினும் வேதம் விளங்கவே
வேதம் ஓதினும் வேதியனாகிலன்
வேதம் ஓதினும் வேதம் மெய்ப்பொருள் காட்டவே"

– Thirumular – Thirumanthiram

Meaning is that
Scriptures are not just for reading and becoming a preacher but to understand the real meaning of the scriptural words to gain the Truth.

வேதம் ஆகமங்கள் இறை நூலாம்
வேதம் ஓதும் போது பொது மற்றும் சிறப்பு பொருள் உண்டு
வேதம் ஓதும் போது இரண்டு அர்த்தம் பேதமே என்பர் சிறியோர்
பெரியோர்க்கு அபேதமே"

– Thirumular – Thirumanthiram

Meaning is that
The scriptures and religious practices (Agamam) are about God but they have double meaning, as if one is general and the other is special. Experienced scholars have known the fact but others (ordinary people) will not accept it.
(He who can understand the special meaning can get the Wisdom).

4. FIVE ELEMENTS

"கண் நாக்கு மூக்குச் செவி ஞானக்கூட்டத்துட் பண்ணாக்கி நின்ற பழம்பொருள் ஒன்று உண்டு
அண்ணாக்கின் உள்ளே அகண்ட ஒளிகாட்டிப் புண்ணாக்கி நம்மைப் பிழைப்பித்த வாறே".

Through Eye, tongue, nose and ear
And the organ Intellect
There is an Ancient One (the Light) that pervades the palatal cavity and it saves us.
The Light which is inside of us goes to the palatal cavity –the junction of the eye, tongue, nose, ear and saves us when danger arises.

We have seen many arts like sculpture, paintings whether it is from East or West, there will be some symbols like women, wings, mirror, soul, half-naked women, white dresses, clouds etc. They just represent the Kundalini energy and its movement.

"கோபுரம் ஐந்து உள கோபுர வாசல் மூன்று உள கோவில் அடைக்க கதவு இரண்டுள கதவிரண்டையும் திறந்து கும்பிட வல்லார்க்கு கோயிலில் குடி இருந்தானே"

– *Thirumular*

There are five towers (five elements) in the temple (our body); there are three gates (fire, water and air); there are two doors (left nostril and right nostril) to open the sanctum sanatorium. He who can open the doors can see the God who resides there.

5. KUNDALINI ENERGY

Kundalini is a broad term for Gundam.

Kundalani Raising

serpent and eagle resemblance to Kundalani Awakening

Om Gundam is kindled fire. We have such a structure in our abdomen.

Kundalam is a type of earring for women. It makes a sound when the wearer moves. So, it is called Kundalani (female character).

The sound from the abdomen is compared to this earring. Hence it is called "Kundalini".

The word is used in yogic texts written in India because this earring is worn mainly by women in India.

Thus, the hot air from the abdomen rises up and goes all over the body giving energy. This rising is called Kundalini rising.

When the mind is calm, the Kundali functions will be in proper condition. That is why calming the mind is advised by scholars who have written manuscripts regarding yoga.

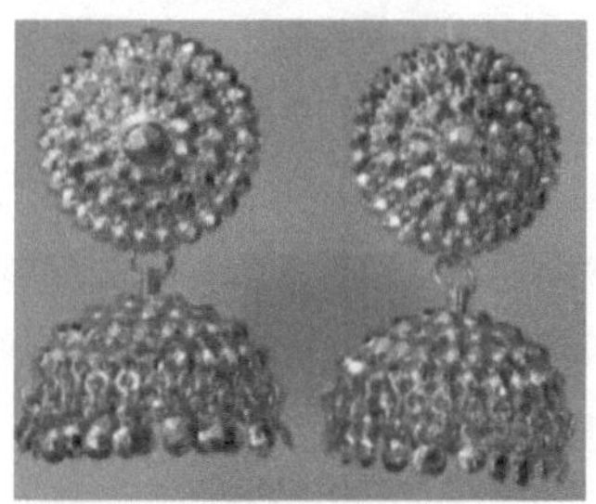

Breathing – Muladhara to Sahasrara

> "அகர முதல எழுத்தெல்லாம் ஆதி பகவான் முதற்றே உலகு" – *Thirukural – Thiruvalluvar*
>
> *The birthplace of all the letters is Muladhara (the lower abdomen). The sound (energy) is generated by the two opposite forces of fire and water.*
>
> *Athi – female – water – moon – -ve charge*
> *Bahavan – Male – fire – Sun – +ve charge*

The vital energy is produced with the reaction of fire and water. This vapour is called "spirit" – ஆவி, உயிர் மூச்சு, life force etc.

"அவன் அவள் அது என்னும் அவை மூவினையில் தோன்றிய திதியே ஒடுங்கி மலத்துளதாம் அந்தம் ஆதி என்மனார் புலவர்."

– Siva Ghana Botham

Meaning is that
The universe is made by He, She and It.

– Siva Ghana Botham…
– Saint Meykanda Nayanar.

He – அவன் – ஆண் – நெருப்பு – Sun – +ve charge
She – அவள் – பெண் – நீர் – moon – -ve charge
அது -(product produced by the water and fire) – vapour, spirit, life force, body's vital energy.

"நாபியின் கீழே நல்லதோர் எழுத்துண்டு பாவிகாள் அதன் பயன் அறிவாரில்லை ஓவியராலாலும் அறிய வொண்ணாது தேவியும் தேவனும் திகழ்ந்திருந்தாரே"

– Thirumular – Thirumanthiram

It (sound or vibration – vital energy produced from the lower abdomen – Mulathara) helps in the act of breath retention below the navel region. It is a rare art that helps the practitioner to advance on the Yoga path.

"Without water and spirit, one cannot enter the kingdom of God."

– from Scripture

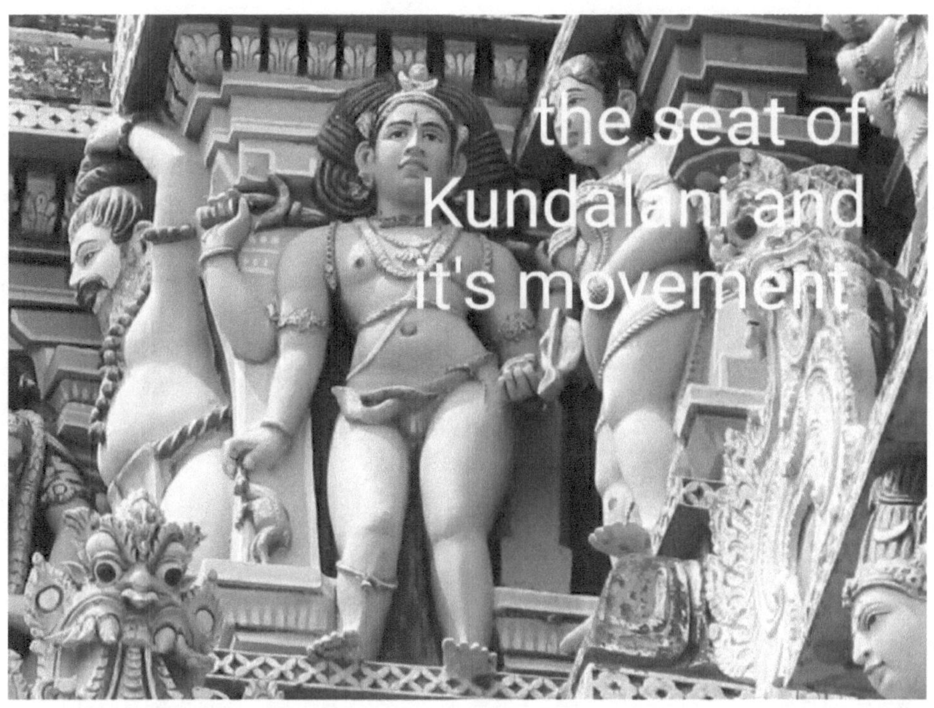
the seat of
Kundalani and
it's movement

"Breathing and
Kundalani
Raising"

"எருவிடும் வாசற் இருவிரல் மேலே
கருவிடும் வாசற் கிருவிரற் கீழே
உருவிடுஞ் சோதியை உள்க வல்லார்க்குக்
கருவிடுஞ் சோதி கலந்து நின்றானே".

(Life force as in the form of light which is generated from the lower part of the abdomen – scrotum)

Two finger length (an inch) above the anus

Two finger length (an inch) below the sex organ,

Lies the Kundalini Fire

If you meditate on the Light

That burns there,

You shall be one with the Lord,

Who all births ends.

Figure 1: Susanna and Elder

Most of the arts like paintings and sculptures may look like nudes, depicting misconduct or misbehaviour with women. But actually, they are different kinds of expression to expose their ideas – sometimes they are attractive while seeing.

> *"The aim of art is to represent not the outward appearance of things, but their inward significance."*
>
> – *Aristotle*

> *"What the superior man seeks is in himself. What the small man seeks is in others."*
>
> – *Confucius.*

The Kundalini Awakening, third eye are one of the subjects of the main subject of The Wisdom. Studying one subject and practising it are two different things. It is like knowing about swimming and practical training in swimming. One who wants to swim, he should have to get in the pool. So, it is an individual's experience.

from East
Susanna and
elders

Figure 1: Kundalini

Raise your breath (Kundalini)".

உண்ணும்போது உயிர் எழுத்தை உயரவாங்கி
உறங்குகின்ற போதும் எல்லாம்
அதுவேயாகும்
பெண்ணின்பாற் இந்திரியம் விடும்போதெல்லாம் பேணி வலம்
மேல் நோக்கி அவத்தில் நில்லு
திண்ணும் காயிலை மருந்தும் அதுவேயாகும்;
தினந்தோறும் அப்படியே செலுத்த வல்லார்
மண்ணூழி காலம் மட்டும் வாழ்வார் பாரு,
மறலி கையில் அகப்படவுமாட்டார்.'

– *Agasthiar*

Raise your breath (Kundalini) when you eat and sleep as well. And when you mate with a woman, keep your breath at the right nostril.
Whatever you eat vegetables and even medicine, raise your breath. If you can do this forever, then you need not worry about death (danger in life).

Figure 1: Kundalini Seat

"இறந்திடும் இருபத்தோராயிரத்துஅறுநூறு பேரும்
இறந்திடில் இக்காயம் போனால் ஈசனைக் காண்பது எந்நாள்
மறந்திடாது அறிவாய்
மூலவாசியை மேலை ஏற்றி
சிறந்த சிற்பரத்து நாகலிங்கரை தெரிசி நெஞ்சே".

You breathe 21,600 breaths per minute. If you could not do so then how do you adore the Almighty? So without fail you should raise your Kundalini and adore him.
(21,600 breaths per day – that is approximately 12 to 15 breaths per minute)

ஏற்றி இறக்கி இருகாலும் பூரிக்குங்
காற்றைப் பிடிக்குங் கணக்கறிவாரில்லை
காற்றை பிடிக்கும் கணக்கு அறிவாளர்க்ககூற்றை உதைக்கும் குறி இதுவாமே.

– Thirumular

No one knows the knowledge of breath (how much time to inhale, exhale and retain the air we breathe). Those who have the knowledge can know how to avoid death when it comes nearby.

'கணக்கறிந்தார்க் கன்றிக் காணவொண்ணாது
கணக்கறிந்தார்க் கன்றிக் கைகூடா காட்சி
கணக்கறிந்து, உண்மையைக் கண்டுகொண்டு நிற்கும் கணக்கறிந்தார், கல்வி கற்றறிந்தோரே.'

Without knowing the knowledge of breath (how many times you breathe per minute) and it's effect on your health, then it is not possible to live a healthy and happy life. Only those who have the knowledge are really educated.
Numbers Are The Highest Degree Of Knowledge. It Is Knowledge Itself."

– Pythagoras

"God Built The Universe On Numbers"

– *Pythagoras*

Shortness of breath

When you have shortness of breath, you feel as though you can't catch your breath. You feel as though you can't have enough air in your lungs. And to try it, breathe deeply. You may also feel a tightness in your chest.

Shortness of breath is the feeling that you cannot get enough air into your lungs. Sometimes, the feeling is when you are physically active or when you lie down flat. You may have other symptoms such as cough or fever.

When you have shortness of breath, it is hard or uncomfortable for you to take the oxygen your body needs. You may feel as if you are not getting enough air. Sometimes, you can have mild breathing problems because of a stuffy nose or intense exercise.

After realizing the importance of the theory, ancient scholars decided to record them permanently in all forms. Their main choices were in written form, sculptures, paintings etc. The temple was considered the right place.

Anyone can see these wherever they look at the temple. Every nook and corner of the temple will expose the great truths.

Pillars, corridors, doors, and walls are some examples. One can see that the Temple Tower which is full of colourful sculptures is nothing but explaining that what is the Truth.

hundreds of sculptures in the temple tower explain single concept of what is within us.

Raise the
Kundalani energy
free Muladhara
to
Sahasrara

Life is Breath. No breath, no life.

Though breathing is spontaneous, sometimes it would get into some trouble. He who wants to know about the troubles and avoid the problems should know the theory of "Weekly String".

Our breath and speech are interrelated. We cannot speak when we inhale the air. So our speech occurs when exhaling the air. It means that the sound is produced at the meeting place of inhaling and exhaling air.

One can see that many sculptures are in nude form. In Tamil language 'Nirvana' means 'Nude'. Here, Nirvana or Nude means leaving off all desires of worldly life (materialism).

It is not what we call "Obscene". Here, nude means what is within us (spirit or soul), not the outward physical body which is a temporary subject.

Temples were built under the supervision of the king and religious leaders. Without their knowledge, no one could make such nude structures like sculptures. It was allowed because there was a purpose in it.

Temples are full of sculptures – some nude and others about Gods and goddesses.

In the same way, in the Western world, paintings were made. Ancient artists have made their work with an impression (formless) of anything in the world that has no form – impermanent. The formlessness has been insisted upon and explained as nudes. Nudes or Nirvana allegorically exposed the real nature of the world. So it is called as Reality, Wisdom, the Truth etc.

"He who says God exists, for him it is existing. he who says as there is no God, for him it is not."

According to Hermetic principles, we are just mind which is no form but formless. The mind will go wherever it wants to go. It is like a flying object.

Dress or attire is for outward showing. It is of no use for life (inside). When life is not, what is the use of the dress?

"If the disguise started in the body when the body dies, then the disguise will also die.

He who does not realize the truth of life is like a log caught in the sea."

The principle of Uniting the physical body and the subtle body is called Yoga. Without knowing this knowledge of yoga there will be no use for doing yoga.

Our breathing is like a string, every breath you take is your life. At some point that string will break, which is a dangerous thing in your life.

Is breathing a conscious or unconscious process?

When we observe every movement, we will become conscious. Because the consciousness itself is related to breath, it is easy to become aware or conscious.

In fact, no one knows from where the consciousness is coming, some say from brain, heart etc.

Hemisphere

Any circle drawn around the earth divides it into four equal halves called hemispheres. But generally, it is divided into Northern hemisphere and Southern hemisphere.

In our body itself, it is the brain – the cerebrum is divided by deep longitudinal fissures; the two hemispheres and callosum are connected.

The right hemisphere controls the muscles of the left side of the body and the left hemisphere controls the right side of the body.

The left hemisphere is responsible for language and speech and is called the 'dominant' hemisphere, as it plays a large part in the body and interprets everything.

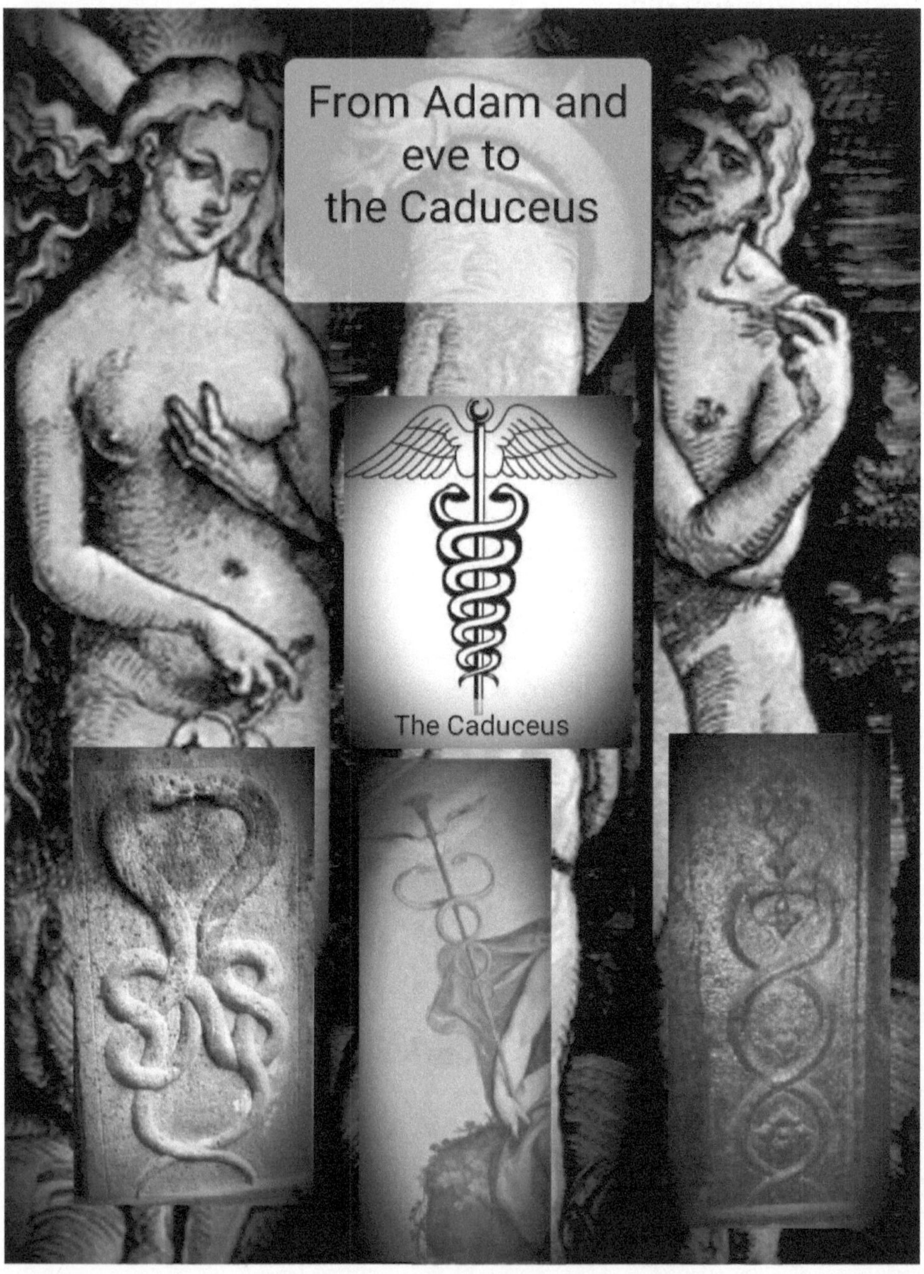

At any given moment you are breathing through one dominant nostril; then sometime later you switch to another one.

It seems to be controlled by the central nervous system.

When the sympathetic system is dominant on the right side and the parasympathetic system is dominant on the left, you get:

Right nostril dominance. Right side of the body may feel it. There will be changes in heart rate, blood pressure, respiration rate and even body temperature.

When the Left nostril dominates

Left side may feel the same and body chemistry and other parameters may change.

When the breath is happening through both nostrils, it is called "Sushmuna". At that time, the vital energy moves through the central nervous system and one can feel comfort and calmness.

Thiruvalluvar, the great saint, quotes some points about the breathing pattern and its effect as follows;

> சமன் செய்து சீர்தூக்கும் கோல் போல் அமைந்த ஒருபால்
> கோடாமை சான்றோர்க்கு அணி.
>
> – *Thirukural*

Sushmuna nadi (not pingala and ldagala nadi – left nostril breath and right nostril breath but through both nostrils) ensures one's good health as balance is maintained and is considered as a measure for good health.

> அருட்செல்வம் செல்வத்துள் செல்வம் – பொருட்செல்வம் பூரியார்
> கண்ணும் உள.
>
> – *Thirukural*

> *Blessing is with the people who can easily breathe in (inhale more air), which can be seen in their shining eyes.*

> நுண்மை நூல்பல கற்பினும் மற்றும் தன் உண்மை அறிவே மிகும்.
>
> – *Thirukural*

Though we read many good books, there is no use, unless we know ourselves.

> அருளில்லார்க்கு அவ்வுலகம் இல்லை – பொருளில்லார்க்கு
> இவ்வுலகம் இல்லாகி யாங்கு. – *Thirukural*

He who has more money would enjoy the worldly life, but he who has more blessings can enjoy the other worldly life (peaceful life in his whole life, even in his old age).

When ancient scholars explain Truth or Wisdom they are sometimes told as funny stories and sometimes in sincere tone.

A common idea among scholars around the world was about nature and its relation to human beings.

Truth or Wisdom or Reality is one (single idea or concept) and it was accepted by all the scholars throughout the world. So, the Truth was explained by ancient scholars in different ways or tastes depending upon the region and its culture and the language.

Truth is one and only like the Sun which is common to all the regions of the earth.

The book is not about devotion, spirituality, or karma, but about the Truth.

Ancient arts and manuscripts are the best sources to realize the Truth.

There are many religions and scriptures. People are following any one of them or none.

But unfortunately, both miss something about Nature or personal life just because of just simply following or not following – as an atheist or theist.

No one can explain the scriptures to be understood and accepted by all people. So there are different opinions among the people.

Five Kosha (Five Levels)

1. அன்னமயம் (Digestive system)
2. பிராணமயம் (Vital energy generated)
3. விஞ்ஞானமயம் (Chemical Changes)
4. மனோமயம் (Mind)
5. ஆனந்தமயம் (Blissful State)

The above-mentioned order is important and should be maintained like the order in seven chakra – Mulathara to Sahasrara.

If we do not have the right food at the right time, then the digestive system will be disturbed.

If our diet is right, then almost all the other levels would be normal and one can feel the blissful state.

> "உன்னும் அளவில் உணரும் ஒருவனைப்
> பன்னு மறைகள் கூறும் பரமனை என்னுள் இருக்கும்
> அணையா விளக்கினை
> அன்னமயம் என்று அறிந்திருந்தேனே"
>
> – *Thirumular*

> *Meaning is that*
> *I have known that the Digestive System where the burning fire and it is also called as the (God as described by ancient scriptures).*
> *"Belly is the real commander of our Body."*
>
> – *Homer*

"கொல்லன் உலை போல கொதிக்கதடி என் வயிறு
நில் என்று சொன்னால் நிற்குதில்லையே
நில்லென்று சொல்லி நிலை நிறுத்த கூடுமாயின்
கொல்லென்று வந்த காலனும் குடி ஓடிப் போகானோ என்
கண்ணம்மா"

Meaning is that
My stomach is boiling like a blacksmith's furnace. The stomach doesn't listen to my words to slow it down. If I could do the same then the demon (death) would not come to me.

"எங்கே இருக்கினும் பூரி இடக்கையிலே
அங்கே அது செய்ய ஆக்கைக்கு அழிவில்லையே அங்கே
பிடித்தது விட்டளவும் செய்ய
சங்கை குறித்த தலைவனுமாமே"

– *Thirumular*

Meaning is that
Wherever you are, breathe through the left nostril. If you could do so, then your body will not perish. It means that God resides within you.

Snakes

Bird

Flying

are the important symbols to understand the Truth

6. SEEING THE THIRD EYE

"Third Eye Opening"

Actually, "third eye opening" is not the right word. Instead, we should say, "Third Eye Seeing".

Each and every one has the third eye and all are eligible to see the same.

Just seeing the third eye will not add any financial or social status.

One can see the third eye when he or she is in a calm mind. Usually, midnight is the right time to see it.

When the normal eyes are opened, we cannot see the third eye (the Light). So, midnight is preferable to see the Light.

Seeing the third eye means that the person is in a calm mind. In the same way, the Kundalini energy moves high when one's mind is calm.

Third Eye – Pineal Gland

Pineal gland

The Light from Muladhara to Sahasrara

Seeing the Third Eye

The main function of the Pineal gland is to follow the natural state of the light and dark cycle from the environment and convey this to the brain, and produce and secrete the hormone melatonin.

The common symptom of the Pineal gland is an alteration in the circadian rhythm, meaning that we may sleep too little or too much, be restless in the night or fall asleep at unusual times.

Melatonin controls the day and night sleep pattern. It is an alkaloid substance.

> "உள்ளத்துளே உளது பல தீர்த்தங்கள்
> மெல்லக் குடைந்து நீராடார் – வினைகெட
> பள்ளம் மேடு அலைந்து திரிவரே
> கள்ள மனமுடையோர் கல்வி இல்லாரே."
>
> – *Thirumular*

All the glands which are beneficial for us are inside of our body. Without carefully secreting it, they wander around here and there (temples) to wash away their sins.

The Pineal gland is key to the body's internal clock because it regulates the body's circadian rhythm and all feelings.

A tiny endocrine gland is in the middle of the brain and controls all the other glands.

Why the Pineal gland is called the 'Third Eye'?

The name "Third Eye" comes from the Pineal gland's primary function of letting in light and darkness as our normal eyes do.

The size of the gland is 100 to 150 mg.

The sympathetic nervous system, parasympathetic and central nervous systems play a very important role in all body functions.

The sympathetic system controls 'fight or flight' response. In other words, this system prepares the body for strenuous physical activity.

The parasympathetic system regulates 'rest and digest' functions.

The Sympathetic Nervous System governs the fight or flight response while the Parasympathetic Nervous system controls the 'rest and digest' response.

Central Nervous System – It is the body's processing centre. The brain controls most of the functions of the body including awareness, movements, speech and the five senses of seeing, hearing, feeling, tasting, and smelling. The spinal cord is an extension of the brain.

Your breathing is like a string, every breath you take is your life. At some point that string will break, which is a dangerous thing in your life.

Is breathing a conscious or unconscious process?

When we observe every movement, we will become conscious. Because the consciousness itself is coming from the breath and it is easy to become aware or conscious.

In fact, no one knows where the consciousness is coming from, as some say from the brain, heart etc.

Hemisphere

Any circle drawn around the earth divides it into four equal halves called hemisphere. But generally, it is considered to be the Northern hemisphere and Southern hemisphere.

In our body itself, the brain – cerebrum – is divided by deep longitudinal fissures; the two hemispheres and callosum connects the two hemispheres.

The right hemisphere controls the muscles of the left side of the body and the left hemisphere controls the right side of the body.

The left hemisphere is responsible for language, and speech and is called the 'dominant' hemisphere. It plays a large part of the body and interprets everything.

In short, practising of Kundalani Awakening and seeing the third eye are just to confirm one's mind's condition. That'll.

The Third Eye is not like the normal eyes. We cannot see the light (third eye) when we open our eyes.

Anybody can see the light in between our eyebrows when our mind is calm and in a dark room or in less light.

Whatever we want to achieve like seeing the third eye, raising the Kundalini.... We have to keep our minds in a calm state.
The purpose of these practices is to keep our mind calm.

"நெற்றிக்கு நேரே புருவத்திடை உற்றுற்று பார்க்க ஒளி விடும் மந்திரம்
பற்றுக்கு பற்றாய பரமன் இருந்த இடம் என்று அறிந்து கொண்டேனே"

– *Thirumular*

Meaning is that
Between the two eyebrows, I have seen the Light and have known that it is the seat of God.

Seeing the Third Eye

Pineal gland

The main function of the Pineal gland is to sense the light and dark cycle from the environment and convey this to the brain, and produce and secrete the hormone melatonin.

The common symptoms of Pineal gland is an alteration in the circadian rhythm, meaning that we may sleep too little or too much, be restless in the night or fall asleep at unusual times.

Melatonin controls the day and night sleep pattern. It is an alkaloid substance.

The Pineal gland is key to the body's internal clock because it regulates the body's circadian rhythm and all feelings.

This tiny endocrine gland is in the middle of the brain and controls all the other glands.

Why the Pineal gland is called as the Third Eye?

The name 'Third Eye" comes from the Pineal gland's primary function of letting in light and darkness as our normal eyes do.

The size of the gland is 100 to 150 mg. But it controls the whole body through other glands and its secretion of necessary hormones.

The sympathetic nervous system, parasympathetic and central nervous system are very important for all body functions.

The sympathetic system controls 'fight or flight' response. In other words, this system prepares the body for strenuous physical activity.

The parasympathetic system regulates 'rest and digest' function.

The SNS governs the fight or flight response while the PNS controls the 'rest and digest' response.

CNS – It is the body's processing centre. The brain controls most of the functions of the body including awareness, movements, speech and the five senses of seeing, hearing, feeling, tasting and smelling. The spinal cord is an extension of the brain.

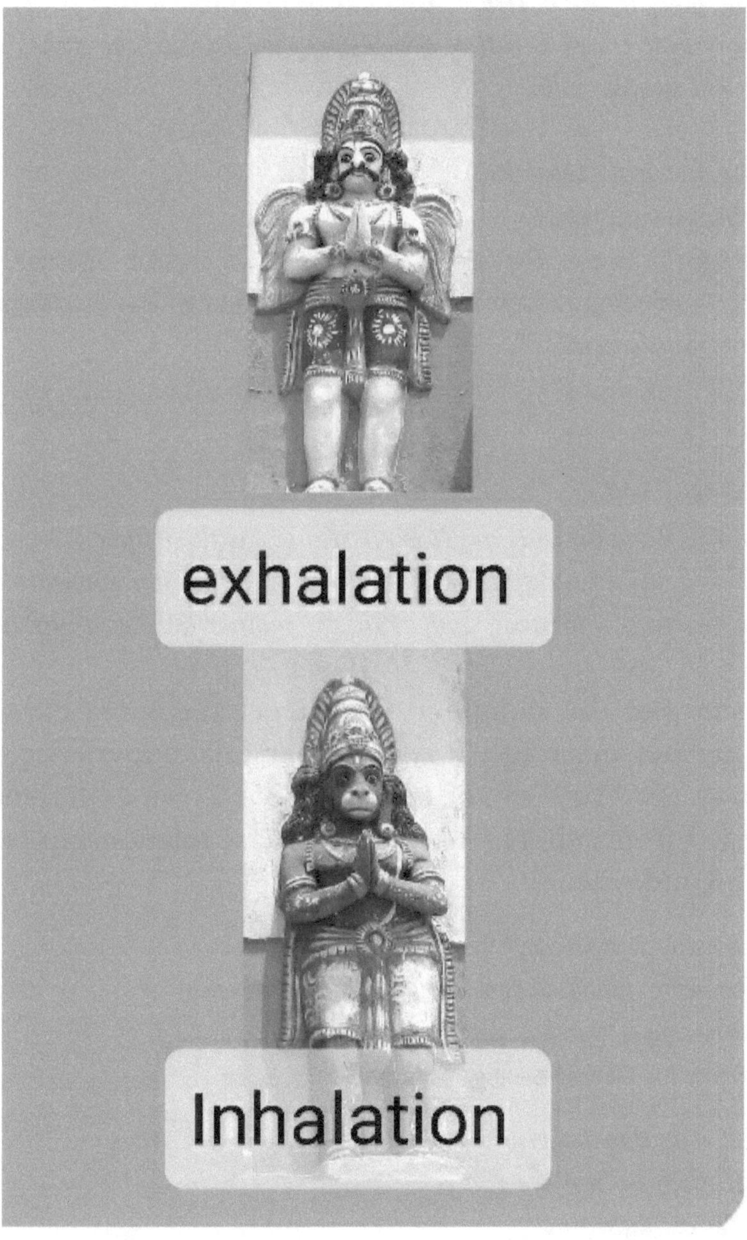

The temple tower is also built in the same concept as the right and left hemispheres.

> "ஊனுடம்பே ஆலையம், உள்ளமே பெரும் கோவில்".
>
> *"Our body is like a Temple and our mind is like a Big Temple." The temple tower is full of sculptures that explain the same. They are not simple dolls.*
>
> முகத்தில் கண் கொண்டு
> பார்க்கும் மூடர்காள்
> அகத்தில் கண் கொண்டு பார்ப்பதே ஆனந்தம் தன்மகட்கு தாய் தன் மணாளனோடு கூடி ஆடிய சுகத்தை சொல் என்றால் சொல்வது எங்கனே".
>
> – *Thirumular*
>
> *Meaning is that*
> *Fools will see the outside. It is blissful to see the inside.*
> *When a young daughter asks her mother about her romance with her husband – privacy, how could the mother tell her daughter?*

It means that the daughter should get the same experience only after her marriage. It is just a personal experience. In the same way, the Truth can be known by one's own experience and not heard from others – like the personal relationship between husband and wife.

> எண்ணாயிரத்தாண்டு யோகம் இருக்கினும்
> கண்ணார் அமுதினைக் கண்டு அறிவாரில்லை
> உண்ணாடிக் குள்ளே ஒளியுற நோக்கினால்
> கண்ணாடி போல் கலந்து நின்றானே.
>
> *Well may they practice Yoga for eight thousand years*
> *Still, they see not the Lord,*
> *Sweet as ambrosia*

And dear like the apple of the eye;
But if within you seek Him enlightened
He within you is,
Even as a reflection in the mirror.

Peepal Tree:

In the same way, Peepal tree is one of the important subjects on Truth or Wisdom. – It should be known by own experience.

Not only did Buddha attain enlightenment under the peepal tree, but the Hindu God Dhakshnamurthy is also seated and he preached under the same tree to his disciples.

Peapal tree and Banyan
tree represent the Truth

7. ARTS AND MANUSCRIPTS ARE MISUNDERSTOOD

Form and Formless

God is most of the time mentioned as woman or goddess and with form and without form.
And so physical body and subtle body.
Subtle body sometimes means the air we breathe or spirit.
"I am formless."

– Ramana Maharishi.

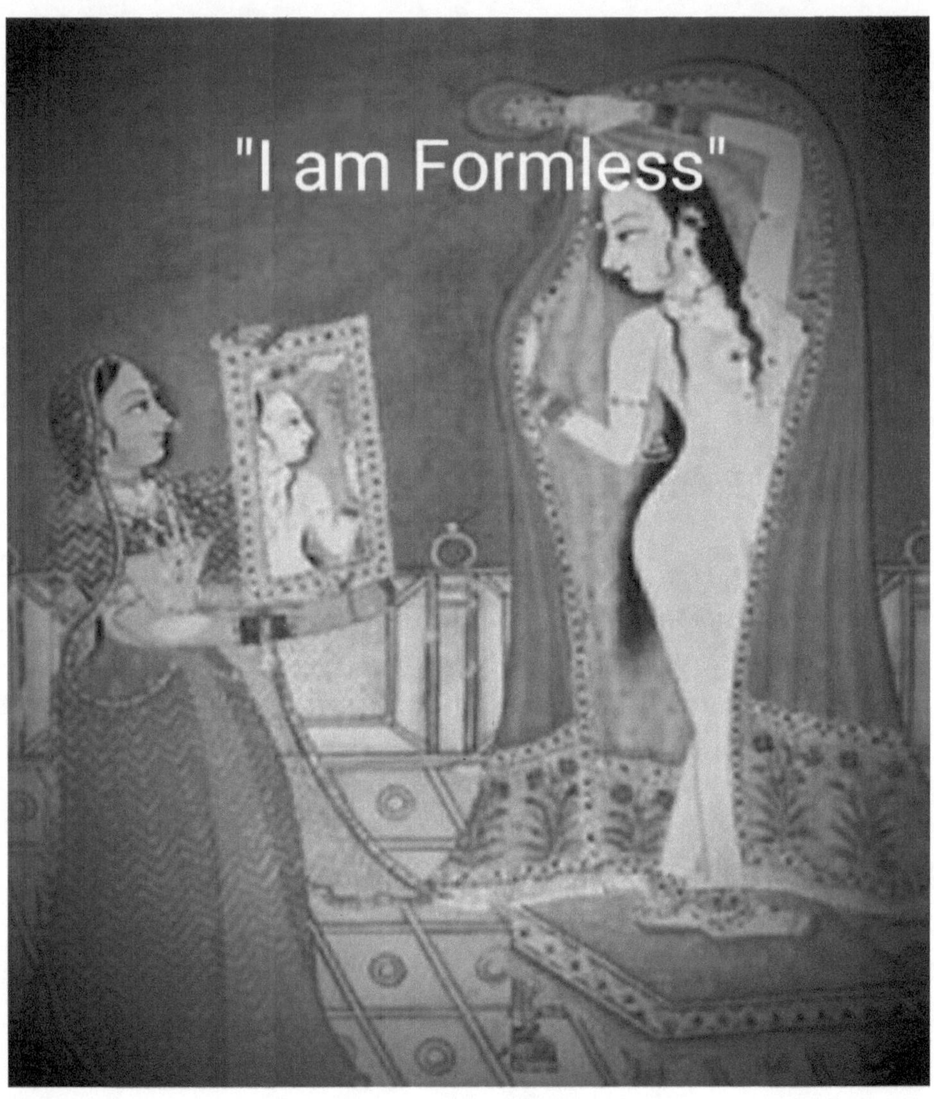
"I am Formless"

Galaxy

Breath and Kundalini

Some important words to think about:

> வானத்தை அண்ணாந்து பார்த்து, பெருமூச்சு விட்டு: "எப்பத்தா" என்றார். அதற்கு திறக்கப்படுவாயாக என்று அர்த்தமாம்.
>
> ***"He looked up to Heaven and with a Deep Sigh said to Him, "Ephphatha!"(which means, "be opened.")***
>
> ***– Bible***

> **இதனையே,**
> கோபுர தரிசனம் மற்றும் கருட தரிசனம் என்று இந்து மதத்தில் கூறப்படுகிறது.

Actually, there is science behind these words.

When we see the sky by bending our neck slightly backwards, then the foodpipe will be tightly closed and the windpipe will be clearly opened. So, breathing will have happened without any disturbance.

"When the neck
is bended, our
body will get
more energy"

We can see the difference before and after doing this. It is an indirect method to encourage us to improve our health.

The picture may be useful for understanding the words.

Here, there are two art works. One is from India and the other is from Greece.

> *Then God said, "Let us make man in our image, according to our likeness, ……so God created man in his own image of God He created him; Male and female and multiply……*
>
> *– from Scripture.*

"Susanna and Elders".

Elders (scholars) wanted to see the life force from Muladhara which is seated in between the anus and the vagina, as the above phrase explained. It is not about sex or any misconduct of the elders with the woman.

Here, the art has been misunderstood.

Some pictures have been shown for….

> *"Art is the queen of all sciences, communicating knowledge to all generations of the world."*
>
> *– Leonardo Da Vinci.*

Raise the Kundalani energy upto
Heart Chakra

- the area where
the Kundalani
energy travels.

The book is not about devotion, spirituality or karma but the Truth.

The Truth comes out from the ancient manuscripts and arts, etc.

There are many religions and scriptures. People are following one of them or none.

But unfortunately, both have missed something because of just following or not following.

No one can explain the scriptures to be understood and accepted by all people. So, there are different opinions among the people.

Generally, every scripture, irrespective of religion, can be classified into three things.

1. Devotion: it is mainly related to Agamas like prayer, singing hymns etc.
2. Karma: Karma means duty. Whether one believes in God or not, he must do his day-to-day work for livelihood. Scriptures referred to duty as personal and social life. That is, what to do and not to do.
3. Wisdom: It is defined by different names as Truth, Reality, Enlightenment etc.

The Truth should be one and it should be irrefutable and accepted by all.

Wisdom is to know the true knowledge of the universe and it's relation to human beings.

It is simple knowledge and all are eligible to understand the Truth.

DEVOTION: At some stage, the devotion will make the devotees doubtful about God's role in their life. So, the devotion sometimes will shake them, particularly when they are met with troubles in their life.

DUTY: Though duty keeps us satisfied most of the time, one day or someday, it would frustrate us, particularly when we are in old age.

WISDOM: Wisdom would relieve us from all the sufferings like old age, diseases, and fear of death.

8. WHAT TO DO TO CORRECT IT

Deep breathing would correct the system.

Right food, right physical and mental activities are important to balance the imbalance.

Confirmation through modern equipment.

These days, there are many household equipment like BP monitors, Oximeter etc.

So, we can check out our body's condition after and before changing the nostrils.

When we are at rest, our pulse rate should be 70 to 75 and the number of breaths 12 to 15 per minute.

Even we can measure this from our wrist with the help of a wristwatch.

"இறந்திடும் இருபத்தோராயிரத்து அறுநூறு பேரும்
இறந்திடில் இக்காயம் போனால் ஈசனைக் காண்பது எந்நாள்
மறந்திடாது அறிவாய் மூலவாசியை மேலை ஏற்றி
சிறந்த சிற்பரத்து நாகலிங்கரை தெரிசி நெஞ்சே"..

You should breathe 21,600 breaths per minute. Otherwise, how could you adore the almighty. So without fail you should raise your Kundalini and adore him.

Some quotes from eminent scholars:

> *"The religion of the future will be a cosmic religion. It should transcend personal God and theology. Covering both the natural and the spiritual, it should be based on a religious sense arising from the experience of all things natural and spiritual as a meaningful unity."*
>
> *– Albert Einstein.*

> *"You were born with wings.*
> *You are not meant for crawling.*
> *So don't.*
> *You have wings.*
> *Learn to use them and fly."*
>
> *– Rumy.*

"Don't you see that they are sliding right when the Sun rises and sliding when the sun sets? This is the best proof for God."
– from Scripture.

....the truth behind the story.

"physical body and the air we breathe should be balanced"

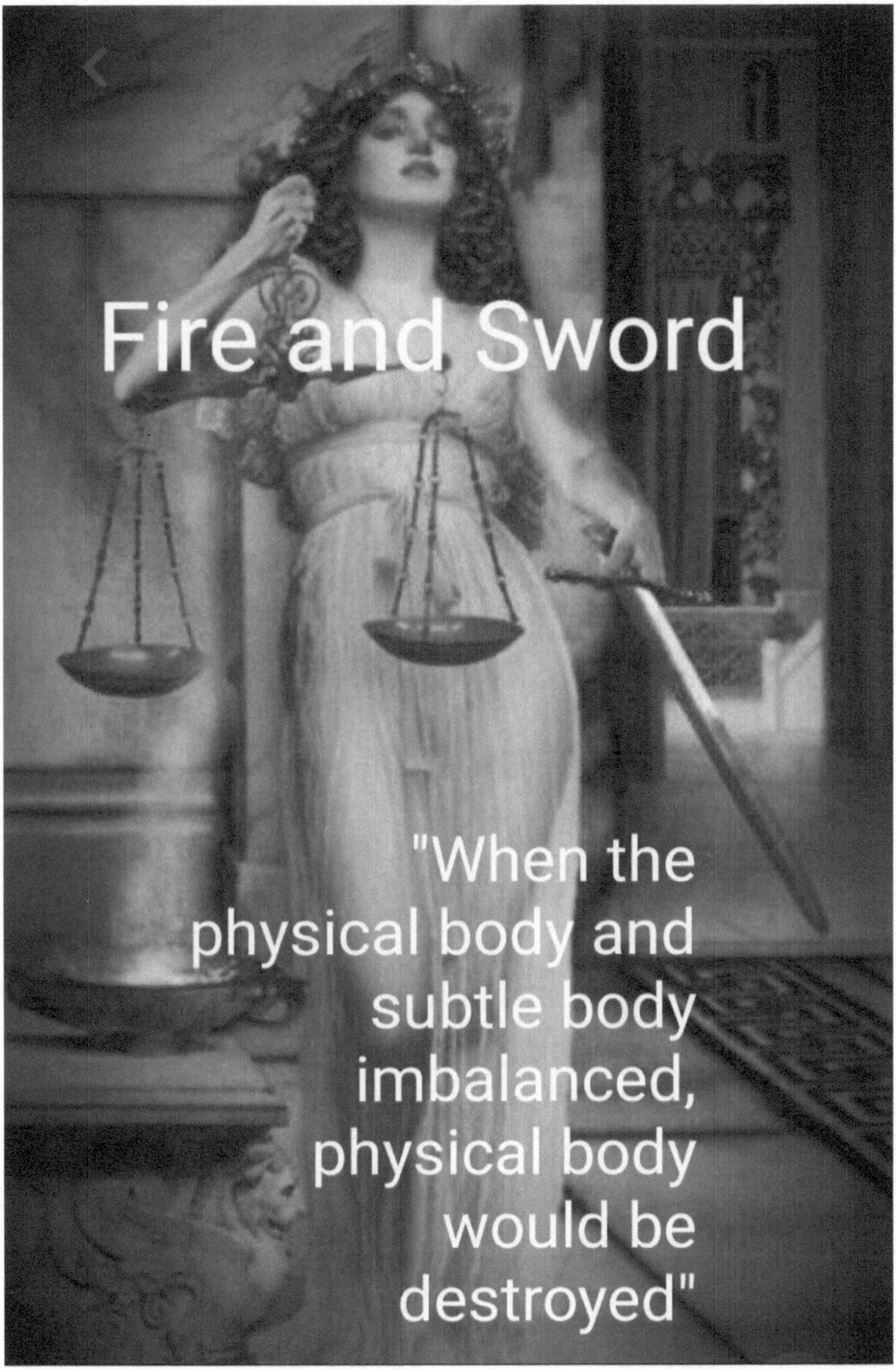

Fire and Sword

"When the physical body and subtle body imbalanced, physical body would be destroyed"

CONCLUSION

"As outside, so inside"

- "Know Yourself"
- "As above, so below"
- "Aham Brhamasmi"
- "God is within us"
- "He is in me, I am in Him"
- "As outside, so inside"
- "Know Yourself"
- "I and Father are one"
- "You are seeking is seeking you"

"Know Yourself"

From Socrates, still the above phrases are questioned, and till today, there is no right answer.

Socrates once said that the unexamined life is not worth living. To examine our life means getting to know ourselves and the world around us better and becoming wiser and better. Knowing ourselves is not of what is outside, but inside.

"The same power that raised Christ from the dead is inside of you."
– Bible.

"The only useful purpose of the present birth is to turn within and realise the Self. There is nothing else to do."
– Ramana Maharishi

One who can get the right answer to any one of the phrases, can get answers for the remaining questions.

Because, all the mentioned phrases are one and the same.

For example, the great Tamil sage Thirumular has said,
"He is suffering because he doesn't know himself; one he who can know himself then he can get relieve from the sufferings; after knowing the self as if how to know that; I am praying myself. "

It means that he has seen the God within him. So, he does pray to himself.

What he is saying is that, everyone should see the self within them. It is a very difficult one.

"I am formless."
– Ramana Maharishi

The "I am...." is a very popular phrase and one of the most conflicting and tricky words.

One who wants to understand the scripture, must imagine as if he or she is the hero of the story.

Here, another phrase may help us to understand what Thirumular achieved.

"As outside, so inside."

We are seeing the outside but cannot see the inside because what we are seeing outside is Maya or Illusion. So, once we come out from the Maya then it would be very easy to see the inside.

> "மனமது செம்மையானால் மந்திரங்கள் செபிக்கவேண்டா
> மனமது செம்மையானால் வாசியை உயர்த்த வேண்டாம்
> மனமது செம்மையானால் வாசியை நிறுத்த வேண்டாம்
> மனமது செம்மையானால் எல்லாம் செம்மையாமே"
>
> – *Agasthiar*

> *Meaning is that*
> *If our mind is perfect, then we need not chant any mantra;*
> *If our mind is perfect, then we need not raise our Kundalini energy (puragam);*
> *If our mind is perfect then we need not retain the Kundalani (retention of breath);*
> *If our mind is perfect then everything will be perfect.*

Maya means illusion. He sees the unreal as real and the real as unreal. Because his mind was trained so from childhood.

So, if we want to know the Truth we should forget what was learned till the present.

Silence and solitude would help to achieve the same and so many changes in our life.

Here, two important things are insisted.

1. We need a calm mind. Ultimately, keeping up a calm mind is emphasised by the ancient sages. If one can achieve the same, then he need not want to do yoga and think about Kundalini, Third Eye opening, etc.
2. Knowing the Truth (just the knowledge) would give relief from all the worldly sufferings.

So, when the above-mentioned two factors coincide, then anyone can live a peaceful life.

When the mind is still and stable, breathing will be calm and the body becomes stable and healthy. The mind is the controller of all the senses. When all the senses are in control, one can feel the inner peace.

> *"Peace is the inner nature of the human being. If you find it within yourself, you will find it everywhere."*
>
> *– Ramana Maharishi*

> *"Happiness is your true nature. It is not wrong to desire it. What is wrong is seeking it outside when it is inside."*
>
> *– Ramana Maharishi*

We know that the Five elements are outside and we cannot control the same. In the same way, five elements are within us and they control us.

We wrongly think that we control ourselves but in reality, the five elements that control us inside are the same Five elements outside that control the outside.

So hereby, the author insists that Our Life Is Predetermined.

More examples from Thirukural:

Thirukural is composed by the Tamil sage Thiruvalluvar. It is also one of the Vedas. Every verse has dual meaning and it would be very interesting to read when we understand its different meanings.

Love Within Us

> "அன்பகத்தில்லா உயிர் வாழ்க்கை வன்பாற்க்கண்
> வற்றல் மரந்தளிர்த் தற்று."

Living alive without moisture in the chest is like a palm tree sprouting in the middle of a desert. The idea is that there is no benefit to anyone.

> "புறத்துறுப் பெல்லாம் எவன்செய்யும் யாக்கை
> அகத்துறுப்பு அன்பிலவர்க்கு".

What good is it to be outwardly full and glitzy and ostentatious for those who are unloved inwardly? What benefit will it bring to others?

> "அன்பின் வழியது உயிர்நிலை அஃதிலார்க்கு
> என்பு தோல் போர்த்த உடம்பு"

Living to love means being alive. Life without it is like skin wrapped around bones.

கண்ணோட்டம்
(Perception)

> "கண்ணோட்டத் துள்ளது உலகியல் அஃதிலார்
> உண்மை நிலைக்கு பொறை."

It is because of love that life takes place here. So, he who is without it is alive and has no benefit other than being burden to the earth.

> "கண்ணிற்கு அணிகலம் கண்ணோட்டம் அஃதின்றேல்
> புண்ணென்று உணரப்படும்."

The most beautiful to the eye is perspective – love. He who does not have it is not an eye. It should be known that it is sore.

> "கருமம் சிதையாமல் கண்ணோட வல்லார்க்கு உரிமை உடைத்திவ்
> வுலகு."

Ancients, particularly Egyptians believed the Eyes are an important indicator of our health, as is Left and Right side nostril breathing.

Eye of RA/RE	Eye of THOTH

Right Eye	Left Eye
Sun related Masculine Yang energy	Moon related, Feminine, Yin energy
Explorer of reasons, mathematics, logic and language	Explorer of nature, emotion sexual activities, intuition, magic
Symbol of Good Luck	A symbol of healing power & Protection

Serpent and eagle
both are enemies but
both have to live
It is the symbol of how
Kundalani raises

God is within us.

We are created in the Image of God. When God is inside us, we cannot do anything ourselves except through God.

> *"I cannot do anything by myself. I am doing what God is doing."*
> *"The world is made up of three things: He, She, and It."*
>
> – *Siva Gnana Botham.*

What's inside is like what's outside.

What is within us is like what is outside of us.

These are some examples of tricky words from the scriptures.

> ஒத்தது அறிவான் உயிர் வாழ்வான் மற்றையான்
> செத்தாருள் வைக்கப்படும்.
>
> – *Thiruvalluvar*
>
> *He who knows how the body and pranic energy are related to the law of nature and how to escape from danger, will live a safe life. All others would be considered as dead persons.*
>
> உவப்பத்தலை கூடி உள்ளப்பிரிதல்
> அனைத்தே புலவர் தொழில்.
>
> – *Thirukural*
>
> *It is a common practice that the scholars would meet and discuss about their writings and would apart happily without any aversion. Actually, ancient scholars had no religion, race, culture.... But their interest was only on the subjects related to Truth or Wisdom.*
>
> செயற்கை அறிந்த கிடத்தும் உலகத்து
> இயற்கை அறிந்து செயல்.
>
> *Nature is our real master. Though we enjoy the artificial things, we should not forget nature.*

எதிரதாக் காக்கும் அறிவினார்க்கு இல்லை
அதிர வருவதோர் நோய்.

Lettered people would have the knowledge of counter actions (breathing pattern against normal), so they can easily find out it and avoid the danger from death because of diseases.
"Art should comfort the disturbed and disturb the comfortable."
– Cesar A. Cruz.

"The noblest pleasure is the joy of understanding."
– Leonardo da Vinci.

Knowing the Kundalini Energy, Seeing the Third Eye, and getting Wisdom won't give us any material benefits but peace of mind.

"Our ancients tell us what is best, but we should learn the modern and choose what is the fittest."
– Benjamin Franklin.

Nothing is equal to peace of mind.

www.ingramcontent.com/pod-product-compliance
Lightning Source LLC
LaVergne TN
LVHW041122150826
845673LV00007B/2156

* 9 7 9 8 8 9 0 6 6 7 7 7 9 *